HEM OF HIS GARMENT

ISBN: 9798660041570

A Publication of Tall Pine Books

|| *tallpinebooks.com*

*Printed in the United States of America

HEM OF HIS GARMENT

DION DIMOLA

Tall Pine

CONTENTS

Acknowledgements   vii
Introduction   ix

 1. I Am Willing   1
 2. Atonement   7
 3. Communion   15
 4. The Word   23
 5. Faith   27
 6. Worship   37
 7. In the Name of Jesus   43
 8. Baptism of the Holy Spirit   53
 9. Prayer   59
10. Words of Knowledge   73
11. Word of Wisdom/Acts of Obedience   79
12. How to Keep Your Healing   85
13. Testimonies   89

Conclusion   105
About the Author   109

ACKNOWLEDGEMENTS

First, I want to thank Jesus! Who gave His life for us. Who gave His blood and His body so we could be forgiven and made whole. I want to thank the Father who gave His Son so our relationship could be restored with Him, whom we will now spend eternity with.

I want to thank every preacher, every pastor, every teacher, every person who has ever stood on and for the Word of God concerning healing. Every person who has suffered ridicule, persecution, or mockery because they believed in divine healing. Every person who has stared sickness and death in the face and said, "I believe in miracles! I believe in a miracle working God and I will see the goodness of the Lord in the land of the living." Every brave person who has ever stepped out there in faith to pray for someone who was sick.

I want to thank Kenneth Hagin, John G Lake, Katherine Kuhlman, Benny Hinn, Bill Johnson, Randy Clark, Michael Koulianos, Todd White, Oral Roberts, Kenneth Copeland, Heidi Baker, Smith Wigglesworth, and Reinhard Bonnke. All of whom have had an impact on my life, especially in regards to the areas of healing and miracles.

I want to thank Michael Santiago (michaelsantiago.org) and Tall Pine Books (tallpinebooks.com) for their involvement in the process and publication of this book.

INTRODUCTION

Many years ago, I injured my back working out. For an entire year I went through this excruciating pain. I didn't know where to turn. I went to the doctors and they just tried to give me pain medication, but could not resolve the problem. At the end of this long painful year I'd had enough. I couldn't take it anymore. Depression and frustration had set in. I wasn't wishing to die or anything but I was at my wits end and couldn't take it anymore.

Then one day I walked by this Christian friend of mine and he asked me what was the matter. I told him about my back. He sat me down and began to tell me about Jesus and His ability to heal. At this point I didn't know about Jesus. I wasn't saved and didn't even know what that meant. I was so desperate though and willing to try anything to get out of this pain. After reading a book that this friend had given to me about Jesus, I went back to him for prayer.

After praying for me, I really didn't notice any change in my condition. At about day three, I started to notice a difference in the way that I felt. By day five I was almost 100% pain free. This would change the course of my life completely. I got saved right after this and began to seek this Jesus that had just healed my body. Since the day the Lord healed my body, I have had the honor of seeing hundreds of people healed by the power of God.

I've seen everything from a sore throat healed to inoperable brain tumors and metal disappearing out of people's bodies. All of this was made possible because the heavy and costly price Jesus paid when He gave His body to be broken for ours. He is the Healer just as much as He is the Savior. In this book, I will go through the many truths that the Lord has very mercifully taught me over the years. Some were learned through incredible victory and some were learned through very painful loss and defeat.

The healing ministry is very rewarding as we get to see the joy of people who are made well and at times brought back from the very brink of death. But at the same time, it is very hard as we have to walk through the grief and pain of death when people don't receive healing in their bodies. Why aren't all who we pray for healed? I can't answer that question as I don't know. But we have to be okay with the mystery and the unknown and celebrate the ones who are healed. I know one thing for sure though. God is good.

James 1:17 says "Every good gift and perfect gift is from above, and comes down from the Father of lights, with whom there is no variation or shadow of turning." Everyone who came to Jesus for healing was healed. Not one did He turn away and not heal them. And the Word says that He is the same yesterday, today, and forever. So why aren't all healed? The problem must lie somewhere with us.

The imperfect vessels whom He has chosen to work through. Do I believe that it is possible to get to a place where 100% of the people we pray for get healed? Absolutely! Jesus said that "these works that you see me do, you will do also. And even greater works will you do because I go to the Father." We are filled with the same Holy Spirit that Jesus was filled with when He walked the earth and healed all who came to Him. This being said, I will not relent or give up. I will continue to press in and seek the Lord until

I am in the place where He can use me to the fullest capacity for His glory.

Let me put this out here at the beginning, I am not the healer. Never was, and never will be. There is only one healer. His name is Jesus. He is, He was, and He will forever be the Healer. I am just a child of God. A vessel which He has chosen to work through. For this I am deeply honored and thankful. I am not a special case though. Every born-again child of God has the ability to pray for the sick and see them recover. If you need healing in your body, then read the truths in this book and reach out to Jesus the healer. Touching the *Hem of His Garment,* He shall make you whole. If you want the Lord to use you in the area of healing, then read the pages of this book and step out in faith. You will lay hands on the sick and people shall be made whole! It doesn't matter if you have been born again twenty minutes or twenty years. The Lord can and will use you for His glory. If you will only believe.

> Mark 6:54-56 "And when they came out of the boat, immediately the people recognized Him, ran through that whole surrounding region, and began to carry about on beds those who were sick to wherever they heard He was. Wherever He entered, into villages, cities, or the country, they

laid the sick in the market places, and begged Him that they might just touch the hem of His garment. And as many as touched Him were made whole."

I AM WILLING

First and foremost, we need to know what the will of the Lord is concerning healing.

It's always the will of God to heal. Always...

We have to know this and never allow thoughts into our mind that are contrary to this truth. As soon as we begin to question or reason whether it's God's will to heal in any given situation, our hearts will begin to waver, and unbelief and doubt are the result. God hates sickness and disease. Sickness steals, kills, and destroys. And if I remember correctly, there is another person that has that same resume; the Devil.

The word says in 1 John 3:8 "...For this reason the Son of God was manifested, that He might destroy the works of the Devil." That's pretty clear. And then we read in Acts 10:38 "how God anointed Jesus of Nazareth with the Holy Spirit and with power, who went about doing good and healing all who were oppressed of the Devil, for God was with Him."

The Word of God says that Jesus came that we might have life and life more abundantly. Sickness doesn't sound like abundant life to me. You might say, but doesn't God use sickness to refine us and mature us? Absolutely not! God is a loving, caring, gentle Father, who is kinder than any earthly father could ever be. I don't burn my son's hand with a lighter to teach him not to touch the stove. I don't break his leg to teach him that it's dangerous to play in the street. Sounds pretty absurd to even think of such a thing. Well it's just as wrong to think that our heavenly Father, the Author of life would need to use sickness to teach us something. Jesus healed everyone who came to Him for healing. If it was the Father's will for some to be sick, then that would mean that Jesus was going against the will of God. And we all know that's not true. All Jesus ever did was the perfect will of God.

In Exodus 15:26 the Lord reveals Himself as Jehovah-Rapha. Which means, "the Lord who heals" Here the Lord literally reveals one of His names as the Healer. That means that it is the very nature of God to heal. For God to make someone sick or to leave them sick, is to actually go against His own name and nature. It has always been the nature of God to heal and restore. We see throughout the entire Bible the Lord's ability and willingness to heal. In Matthew 8:2 we see a leper coming to Jesus for the healing of his body. He says in verse 2 "Lord if you are willing You can make me clean" Jesus's immediate response is "I am willing" He touched the leper and he was healed.

Right after this, we see a centurion come to Jesus for the healing of his servant and Jesus said to him *"I will* come and heal him." Then another few verses later we see Jesus enter into Peter's wife's mother's house. She was sick of a fever. Jesus touched her hand and the fever left her. As you see, it was Jesus' heart to heal. Luke 4:18 further reveals God's will concerning healing. It reads "The Spirit of the Lord is upon me because He has anointed Me to preach the gospel to the poor; He has sent Me to heal the brokenhearted, To proclaim liberty to the captives and recovery of sight to the blind, to set at liberty those who are oppressed; to proclaim the acceptable year of the Lord."

John the Baptist later asked his disciples to go ask Jesus if He was the coming one or if they should look for another? Jesus' response was "Go and tell John the things you have seen and heard: the blind see, the lame walk, the lepers are cleansed, the deaf hear, the dead are raised, the poor have the gospel preached to them." The very sign of the coming Messiah was healing, restoration, wholeness and salvation." Luke 19:10 says "for the Son of Man has come to seek and save that which was lost." The Greek word used here for save is *sozo*. Sozo means "To heal, save, deliver. To make well, heal, restore to health. To keep safe and sound, to rescue from danger or destruction." Healing, health, and wholeness will always be the will of God.

Forgive me if I am really hitting this hard here, but this has to be solidified in our hearts. When we know the heart and will of God concerning something, we can then stand in complete agreement with Him in faith. Knowing sickness is an enemy just as much as sin is, we can stand against it. Resisting it and driving it from our lives and the lives of those around us. Sickness does not bring God glory. I have often heard people say that their sickness was bringing God glory because of the way that they were handling it. I have to ask you my friend. Which do you think is bringing God more glory? You embracing that sickness as if it was a gift from God. Or you standing against it and sending that disease back to hell where it came from.

I'm not being insensitive here. Trust me. If you are sick in your body right now, I am so sorry that you are having to go through that. I know what you are going through. I have been on the very edge of death before because of sickness. I have had friends and family members die of sickness. It's a vicious and terrible thing. I am being very direct here because I need you to know the origin of it. Sickness is not a gift from God to make you more like Jesus. You can read through every gospel and not one time will you ever read that Jesus was sick. And not one time will you read of Jesus telling someone that He can't heal them because their sickness was bringing glory to God. It's just not in there.

If our experience isn't lining up with scripture, we don't need to create a doctrine explaining away the lack of breakthrough or power in our life. We should allow it to fuel us to press into God until we see breakthrough and victory. Is it going to be easy? Probably not. But that's why it's called breakthrough. You most likely will have to push through some type of resistance to breakthrough to the other side. Once you get breakthrough though, you will gain an authority and an increase of faith in that area to believe for bigger things.

Let us not stop short of receiving all that Jesus paid for with the giving of His life. He paid a very costly price for us to be healed. God loves you. He cares for you affectionately and watchfully. He knows the very number of hairs on our head. He knows what you are going through. He knows your pain and tears and wants to take that pain away. What loving Father wouldn't want their child healthy? He is willing and able and wants to heal your body today. Turn to Jesus my friend. He is the Bread of Life who came down from heaven, that we might have life and have it more abundantly. Let His words be the final authority in your heart concerning healing, "I Am Willing."

2

ATONEMENT

Now that we have established the will of God concerning healing, I want to show you how the healing of our bodies was actually a part of redemption. Healing was in the atonement. First, we must know how sickness entered into the world. It wasn't in the original design when God created the earth. When God finished His work on the sixth day and rested on the seventh, He looked at all that He had created and said, "It is good". Sickness is not good. So where did it come from?

It entered into the world when Adam sinned. Sickness is directly connected to sin. If there was never any sin, then there would never have been any sickness. God told Adam in the garden of Eden, "Of every tree of the garden you may freely eat; but of the tree of the knowledge of good and evil you shall not eat, for in the day that you eat of it you shall surely die." Well, as we all know, Adam ate from the tree and sin became the door through which death entered the earth. Romans 5:12 says "Therefore, just as through one man, sin entered the world, and death through sin and thus death spread to all men, because all sinned." We see here that death entered the world through sin. Romans 6:23 says "the wages of sin is death."

Sickness and disease, a form of death entered the world through sin. It's basic cause and effect. Sin was the cause and sickness and death was the effect. We know that when Adam ate of the tree, he didn't fall over immediately dead. He died spiritually here, as he didn't die physically for another 930 years. But his sin caused him to be separated from God Spiritually. Losing the nature of God in the process and taking on the nature of the Devil (sin nature). Therefore, God sent him from the garden so he wouldn't eat from the tree of life and live forever in his sinful state. Man was never meant to die. He was created to dwell with God in paradise (Eden), a place of delight and pleasure free from sickness.

But through his rebellion he was forced from his union with God and the tree of life. We see here that Adam was separated from God and anything separated from God is dead or in the process of dying, as God is life. The curse entered the earth as well through Adam's sin. Genesis 3:17 says, "...Cursed is the ground for your sake; In toil you shall eat of it all the days of your life." Then again, we read in Romans 8:20 "For the creation was subjected to futility, not willingly, but because of Him who subjected it in hope; because the creation itself also will be delivered from the bondage of corruption into the glorious liberty of the children of God."

Sickness is a part of the curse. This last verse we just read, talks about creation also being subject to the bondage of corruption. Sickness is bondage and corruption in the body. This passage goes on to talk about the redemption of our bodies. Where our bodies are no longer subject to sickness, disease, or death. O' that will be a glorious day. Thankfully God has made a way for our bodies to be healed and in health as we eagerly wait for that wonderful day. Even though Adam sinned in the garden, God still dearly loved man.

God is a holy God, and a holy God cannot dwell among or walk with sinful man. Something had to be done, so that God could continue to interact with His creation Adam. Therefore, God made atonement for man's sin. Genesis 3:21 says, *He covered Adam and Eve in tunics of skin.* The word atonement means "to cover, to appease, to pardon." God covered man's sin so that He could continue to have fellowship with man until the coming of His Son Jesus. Who would not just cover sin but would completely remove it from man, enabling man and God to be spiritually united again. Sin was the cause of sickness. When God dealt with sin, He also dealt with the effects of sin, which are sickness, disease, and death.

There are many examples in the Old and New Testament tying sin and sickness together and forgiveness and healing. The first example was when the Israelites complained and rebelled against Moses. A plague broke out and Moses said to Aaron "Take a censer and put fire in it from the altar, put incense on it, and take it quickly to the congregation and make atonement for them." When Aaron did this the plague was stopped. Psalm 107 says, "Fools, because of their transgression, and because of their iniquities were afflicted." Psalm 38:3, "There is no soundness in my flesh because of Your anger, nor any health in my bones because of my sin."

In Mark 2:9-12 we have the story of Jesus healing the paralytic man. Let's pick up in verse 9, "Which is easier, to say to the paralytic, 'Your sins are forgiven you,' or to say 'Arise, take up your bed and walk'? But that you may know that the Son of Man has power on earth to forgive sins" He said to the paralytic, "I say to you, arise, take up your bed, and go to your house." Immediately he arose, took up the bed, and went out..." Here is a perfect example of sin/sickness and forgiveness/healing. John 5:14 says, "See, you have been made well. Sin no more, lest a worse thing come upon you." This was the story where Jesus healed the guy at the pool of Bethesda.

Let me point out, I'm not saying that if you are sick right now that you have sin in your life. I am not saying that at all. I'm just showing that sickness entered into the earth because of the original sin committed in the garden. Now at the same time, we have just seen by example that it is possible for sickness in someone's life to be directly related to sin they have committed. Until the final judgment and while we live in this fallen world sickness is going to be around. But I absolutely believe that we can get to a place where we walk above sickness and disease. Where it has no place in our lives and it can't touch us, because we have so much life flowing from us.

Next, I want to look at numbers 21. Here the Israelites spoke against God and Moses. After they spoke against God fiery serpents came out against the Israelites biting them and killing them. This is what they said to Moses, "We have sinned, for we have spoken against the Lord and against you; pray to the Lord that He takes away the serpents from us."

God told Moses to make a Bronze serpent and put it on a pole. Why a bronze serpent? Bronze speaks of judgment. Why put a serpent, the very thing killing them on a pole?

Deuteronomy 21:23 says that everyone hung on a tree is accursed of God. When the Israelites looked at the serpent on the pole, they knew that the thing that was killing them had been judged and cursed by God. As everyone who had been bitten looked at the serpent, they were healed. This was a shadow of Jesus. One day He would be lifted up on the tree of Calvary. John 3:14 says, "And as Moses lifted up the serpent in the wilderness, even so must the Son of Man be lifted up, that whoever believes in Him should not perish." 2 Corinthians 2:21 says that Jesus became sin. "For He made Him who knew no sin to be sin for us, that we might become the righteousness of God in Him".

God judged sin in the body of Jesus and cursed the very thing that was killing us. It goes further than this. Remember that the wages of sin is death, and sickness a form of death was the result of sin. Jesus not only became our sin that it might be judged on the cross but He also bore the punishment or results of that sin which was sickness and death. Isaiah 53:4-5 says, "Surely He has borne our griefs (sickness) and carried our pains of punishment, yet we esteemed

Him stricken, smitten by God and afflicted. He was wounded for our transgressions, He was bruised for our iniquities; The chastisement for our peace was upon Him, And by His stripes we are healed." WOW! Are you seeing this! God is so good. He covered it all.

These very verses were cited in the New Testament when Jesus was healing the sick Matthew 8:16-17 "When evening had come, they brought to Him many who were demon possessed. And He cast out the spirits with a word, and healed all who were sick, that it might be fulfilled which was spoken by the prophet Isaiah, saying: "He Himself took our infirmities and bore our sicknesses."" Jesus is so amazing! He took everything that we were deserving of. Every sickness, every disease, every punishment, and every judgment as our substitute and gave us His health and life.

No greater act of love or mercy has ever been committed that is comparable to what Jesus has done for us. This is why our bodies can be healed, because Jesus paid for that healing with His very own blood and body. His body was broken so that our bodies could be healed. Let me take it one step further or let me say God took it one step further. Remember how I showed you that the curse, (sickness being a part of the curse) entered the world because of sin. Then we saw in Deuteronomy 21 how everyone who hung on a tree is cursed. Jesus bore the curse.

Galatians 3:13 says "Christ has redeemed us from the curse, having become the curse for us (for it is written, "Cursed is everyone who hangs on a tree,") that the blessing of Abraham might come on the gentiles in Christ Jesus." Not only did He take care of sin, sickness, and the curse but the blessing came upon us. Healing, health, and wholeness are a part of that blessing. We have to know these things. They belong to us and Jesus paid a heavy price to give them to us. Sickness has no right to our body! Jesus already bore it for us! We have the right and the authority to tell it to leave!

3

COMMUNION

I NOW WANT TO TOUCH ON THE SIGNIFICANCE AND power of taking communion. Communion is a very intimate meal with God. Communion is a covenant meal. There's life, healing, and strength found in this meal. We are actually partaking of the finished work of Christ every time we partake of this meal. We are partaking of Jesus' flesh when we eat the bread which was broken for our flesh that we might be healed. We are partaking of His blood when we drink the cup, which was shed that our sins might be forgiven.

In 1 Corinthians 11:23-26 Paul goes through the institution of the Lord's supper with the Corinthian church. He says, "For I received from the Lord that which I also delivered to you: that the Lord Jesus on the same night that He was betrayed took bread; and when He had given thanks, He broke it and said, "Take, eat; this is my body which is broken for you; do this in remembrance of Me." In the same manner He also took the cup after supper, saying, "This cup is the New Covenant in my blood. This do, as often as you drink it, in remembrance of Me." For as often as you eat this bread and drink this cup, you proclaim the Lord's death till He comes."

Before Jesus was crucified on the Cross, He was violently scourged by the Roman soldiers. They whipped Him, beating Him until He was unrecognizable. Isaiah 52:14 says that He was marred more than any man. This was the event that Isaiah 53:5 was referring to when it said "He was wounded for our transgressions, He was bruised for our iniquities; The chastisement of our peace was upon Him, And by His stripes we are healed."

Jesus did this for us! His body was broken so our bodies could be healed. When we partake of the bread during communion, we are partaking of His broken body. All our sicknesses and brokenness are transferred to His body and all of His health, strength and wholeness are transferred to our bodies. You may say *how is this possible, this happened two thousand years ago?* It is the same way your sins are forgiven when you ask for forgiveness. Jesus' works are eternal. Time is irrelevant.

This is the same thing which happened when the Israelites partook of the Passover meal before leaving Egypt. They were putting their faith into an event yet to come and we are putting our faith into an event that has already happened. Let us look back to this amazing Exodus of the Israelites from the tyrannical oppression of the Egyptians. This story is recorded in the 12th chapter of Exodus. The tenth and final plague was about to be brought upon the Egyptians. All the firstborn of the Egyptians were to die, but none of the children of the Israelites were to be harmed. But in order for this to happen, they were to take a Lamb and to kill it at twilight.

They were then supposed to take some of it's blood and put it on the doorposts and on the lintel of the houses where they were to eat it. They were to eat the flesh of the lamb on that night; roasted in fire, with unleavened bread. Then God said, "For I will pass through the land of Egypt on that night, and I will strike all the firstborn in the land of Egypt, both man and beast; and against all the gods of Egypt I will execute judgment: I am the Lord. Now the blood shall be a sign for you on the houses where you are, and when I see the blood, I will pass over you; and the plagues shall not be on you to destroy you when I strike the land of Egypt.

So, this day shall be a memorial; and you shall keep it as a feast to the Lord throughout your generations. You shall keep it as a feast by an everlasting ordinance." Do you see that last sentence? An everlasting ordinance! Why everlasting? I will tell you why. Because Jesus is the Passover Lamb! Let us look at this for a minute. They were supposed to take a lamb without blemish. This speaks of Jesus, the perfect Lamb of God. Who was spotless and sinless in every way. Then they were supposed to put the Lamb's blood on the two doorposts and the lintel. Signifying the cross that Jesus was to be hung from. Then they were supposed to roast it in fire until it was black and eat it with bitter herbs. The same way Jesus was stained with our sins and drank from that bitter cup. They weren't supposed to allow any of it to remain until morning. Jesus was pulled from the Cross and not allowed to remain overnight because of custom. Jesus is our Passover Lamb!

Paul said in 1 Corinthians 5:7, "...For indeed Christ our Passover, was sacrificed for us." Then again in John chapter 1 verse 36, John the Baptist said when Jesus walked up, "Behold the Lamb of God!" The power behind the Israelite's Passover meal is the same power behind the meal we partake of during communion. The body and blood of Jesus. God gave and sacrificed His firstborn Son, so they wouldn't have to lose theirs. Not only did they not lose their firstborn, but they were delivered from the captivity of Egypt. The same way that we are delivered from sin, sickness, and the devil when we put our faith in Jesus' sacrifice for us. They left Egypt with riches. The same way that we are born-again into an inheritance in Christ that far surpasses all the riches of this world. Then finally, when they left from Egypt, Psalm 105:17 says, "And there was none feeble among them."

Do you see this? This is amazing! They say about two million Israelites left Egypt that day. Think of the magnitude of this. Out of two million there was not one feeble person among them. It doesn't just say *none sick*. It says *none feeble*. That means none were even weak! Now you know out of two million people, there had to be people all ages. Young, old, and everywhere in between. Why were there none feeble among them? It was because they had just partaken of the Passover meal. As they put the Lamb's blood on the doorposts their sins were atoned for. And as they ate the Lamb their bodies were healed and strengthened. The same way the cup in communion represents the blood of Jesus which was shed for the remission of our sins and the bread represents His broken body. Which was broken so we could be healed.

Communion is a covenant meal. Every covenant is cut with the shedding of blood. A covenant is the most powerful agreement two people can make together. Though it is so much more than an agreement or contract. It is an actual union, bonding and oneness. It is basically saying, you now have access to all that belongs to me. I am no longer my own. God cut a covenant with us! And the blood of Jesus was the blood shed to cut that covenant. God joined Himself to us with an everlasting covenant. An eternal covenant.

Remember Jesus said, "This cup is the New Covenant in My blood." Every time we take communion, we are to remember this covenant that we have with God. God has promised in this covenant to be with us, to provide for us, to lead us, to heal us, to deliver us, to love us, and to protect us. I remember on several occasions when I was stressing over finances or a health issue. The Lord would remind me of this covenant.

He would tell me, "I have bound myself through a covenant to take care of you. I have bound Myself to heal you." A Covenant has been cut. And because of the sacrifice of the body and blood of Jesus, we can be made whole. Take communion often and every time that you take it you know that you are partaking of the body and blood of Jesus, which cleanses us from sin and heals our bodies.

4

THE WORD

Proverbs 4:20-22 "My son, give attention to My words; Incline your ear to My sayings. Do not let them depart from your eyes; keep them in the midst of your heart; For they are life to those who find them, And health to all their Flesh."

THERE IS HEALING IN THE WORD OF GOD. THE BIBLE is a living book. Jesus is the Word of God and as we read and meditate on God's Word, life comes to our spirits, our souls, and our bodies. Psalm 119:50 says, "This is my comfort in my affliction, for Your word has given me life." It is the spirit which provides life to the body. Not the body providing life to the spirit. Your spirit can live without the body, but your body cannot live without the spirit. When we are born again our spirits are connected to the Spirit of God and the Spirit of God is the Spirit of life.

Jesus said in John 6:63 "...My words are spirit, and they are life." When we read the Word of God, we are feeding our spirit man, and as our spirit man gets stronger life flows to our bodies. I don't know if you have ever seen someone who's spirit man is really strong. It almost seems like they glow. There is so much life flowing from them. It is very rare that you will see these individuals get sick. If you do, they do not stay sick long. They are consistently reading the Word of God and feeding on the Bread of Life. I'm not talking about just mindlessly glancing over the words. I'm talking about feeding on the Word. Interacting with the Word and the Holy Spirit as you're reading. Digesting the words.

I know many times in which the Word has brought life to me. I remember one time in particular. I was about to go to bed and all of a sudden, my chest started to feel really tight on one side. To be honest it was a little alarming, but as I lay there, Romans 8:11 came to my heart. "But if the same Spirit who raised Jesus from the dead dwells in you, He who raised Jesus from the dead will also give life and quicken your mortal flesh." I lay there and said that scripture over and over again. Just breaking it down, meditating on it and digesting it.

Then it happened, that scripture got down into my spirit. It was like a flash of lightning. This electricity and energy which came from deep...deep within me. It came out of my spirit. It surged through every cell of my body and went straight to that tight spot in my chest. All the pain and tightness left my chest immediately.

I felt extreme relief as the peace of God settled on me. I rejoiced, thanking the Lord for awhile, and then I fell asleep; sleeping better than I had slept in a long time. Just like the scripture said, my mortal flesh had just been quickened. Have you ever gone to a church service just feeling *down*? But by the time you left, you felt energized and full of life. That's because the Word of God was being preached. I've known people to get healed just sitting listening to the Word being preached. It is life!

Jesus is the Word of God. And as we read and receive the Word, we are actually fellowshipping with and receiving the life of Jesus. We read the logos until we hear the rhema. When you hear the rhema you have found the present voice of God. You are then interacting with the living word in the written word. You have found His presence. You have found the life-giving word. In the word He is saying in that moment, the faith, the grace, and the power is released to bring the fulfillment of that word. The

Bible is a living book. You have to understand, God did not write a book. He spoke a book. And that book is still speaking.

There is so much more power in the word then I think we realize. David said, "I rejoice at Your word as one who finds great treasure" (see Psalm 119). Through the centuries many have bled and died so that we could have a Bible in our hands. Let us treasure and consume it as if our very life depended on it.

It is written, "Man shall not live by bread alone, but by every word that proceeds from the mouth of God". The word brings strength to our spirits the same way that food brings strength to our bodies. Remember what Jesus said, "The words that I speak to you, they are spirit and they are life."

5

FAITH

IN THIS CHAPTER, I WANT TO GO OVER WHAT FAITH actually is. Faith is important, but it shouldn't be our focus. I remember I used to put so much emphasis on trying to increase faith when I should have been focusing on Jesus and developing my relationship with Him. Faith grows as we get to know Jesus more. As our trust and relationship with Him grows our faith grows. Faith comes by hearing and hearing by the Word of God.

Faith is belief and trust in a person; Jesus. It is believing in Him and what He says. When He speaks, we are all faced with a decision. Do we believe Him or not? The more we get to know Him through prayer, through the word, and walking with Him and building history together. The greater our trust and faith will grow. To where we will believe Him faster and for bigger things. The foundation of faith is *relationship*. Jesus is the author and the finisher of our faith. This means when He speaks, or has spoken, concerning something (Author) our hope and belief for that thing is born.

Then we patiently trust, believing He will bring to pass that which He has spoken. He brings it to pass, and we receive what we are believing for (finisher). Our faith starts with Him and ends with Him. I like the beginning of that verse, "Looking unto Jesus, the Author and Finisher of our faith." Looking unto Jesus. Faith is not a one time act but a continuous gazing. Christianity used to be called 'the way' and 'the faith.' Remember Paul said, "I have finished the race, I have kept the faith."

He never turned from looking at Jesus. Faith is in a person. It is belief in the faithful One. Hebrews 11:11 says, "By faith Sarah received strength to conceive seed, and she bore a child when she was past the age, because she judged Him faithful who had promised." We don't put our faith in "our faith or ability to believe for something." We put our faith in Jesus. The woman with the issue of blood who touched the hem of Jesus' garment, wasn't saying over and over again I believe I receive...I believe I receive. Nor was she saying, if I just had enough faith I will be healed.

She said, if I can just get to Jesus. If I can just touch the hem of His garment I will be healed. Her faith was displayed through her coming to Him. Everyone who came to Jesus was healed. It didn't matter if they had little faith or mountain moving faith. If they had enough faith to come to Him for healing. Then He healed every single one of them. It didn't matter what their condition was or how long they had been in that state.

Faith produces corresponding action. Many think they are in faith but their actions or lack of action reveal what they truly believe. Many are just in mental assent. They believe with their mind, but they truly don't believe in their hearts. Faith is of the heart. It isn't of the mind. If I truly believe something there is a rest, a trust, and an action.

That action may be to patiently wait, trusting what God has said will come to pass. Or it may be some type of physical action. Like when God told Noah to build an ark. What did he do? He built an ark. Or when God told Abraham to leave his homeland. What did he do? He left his homeland.

They did these by faith, trusting the One who spoke. One of my favorite people in the bible is Abraham.

He was named the father of faith. Romans 4:19-22 says, "And not being weak in faith, he did not consider his own body, already dead (since he was about a hundred years old), and the deadness of Sarah's womb. He did not waver at the promise of God through unbelief, but was strengthened in faith giving glory to God, and being fully convinced that what He had promised He was able to perform. And therefore, it was accounted to Him for right-eousness." I love this. It is one of my favorite revela-tions of faith.

Let us look at this for a minute. First it says that he considered not his own body. That means that he did not believe what he saw in the natural world over the voice of God. His body may have been saying one thing, but because God had said some-thing different, he believed that instead. He believed the word of the Lord over his symptoms or what his body was telling him. Next, we see that he did not waver at the promise of God through unbelief but was strengthened in faith giving glory to God. Faith rejoices.

If we truly believe that what we have prayed for or what God has said is ours, we would have a heart of thankfulness and praise. It says that he was strength-ened in faith giving glory to God. I promise you, if you are barely hanging on in faith over something, if you will start praising God and thanking Him for it, your faith will strengthen and grow to a place of complete trust and rest. I've known people who had received partial healing in an area of their bodies, but as they began to praise and thank God for healing their bodies. Faith grew and they received complete healing in their bodies. Why did faith grow? Because they began to see God rightly and their trust in His goodness and faithfulness grew. The next verse in this run of verses is probably one of the best definitions of faith.

Verse 21 says, "And being fully convinced that what God had promised He was also able to perform." We must be fully convinced that God is faithful and that He is who He says He is. In Isaiah 46:11 God said, "Indeed I have spoken it: I will also bring it to pass. I have purposed it; I will do it". God is kind, loving, and faithful. He wants you healthy and whole, even more than you want to be healed.

Let us not put our trust in our ability to receive, but in His willingness and ability to give. Put your faith in the Word of God and not your feelings. If we put our faith in Him and His word, we will always be stable standing on the rock. But if we put our faith in our feelings, we will be unstable and waver. Get in the Word of God and spend time with the Lord in prayer. As you get to know Him more, trust will grow in your heart to where you will never have to worry about unbelief again. You'll know Him. You will know because He has spoken, it shall come to pass.

> Hebrews chapter 11:6 "But without faith it is impossible to please Him, for he who comes to God must believe that He is, and that He is a rewarder of those who diligently seek Him."

I want to point out though, I'm not belittling the importance of confession. Confession and speaking the word is very important. Realize though, we don't confess something to try and get ourselves to believe it. That would be trying to get our minds to believe something that we don't actually believe in our hearts. Remember faith is of the heart. If we just confess something over and over again, trying to get ourselves to believe it, we are keeping it in our mind. And that will keep us in an endless cycle of frustration and receiving nothing.

When we make a confession or a declaration, it has to come out of our spirit from a place of conviction in our heart to it's truth. 2 Corinthians 4:13 says, "And since we have the same spirit of faith, according to what was written, 'I believed and therefore I spoke,' we also believe and therefore speak." I want you to notice, it says here that they spoke because they believed and not that they spoke in order to get themselves to believe. If we look at what it says in Mark 11:22-24 we will see this truth plainly. "...Have faith in God. For assuredly, I say to you, whosoever says to this mountain, 'Be removed and be cast in the sea,' and does not doubt in his heart, but believes that those things he says will be done, he will have whatever he says. Therefore, I say to you, whatever things you ask for when you pray, believe that you receive them, and you will have them."

I will tell you a little secret, or key, to this verse. If you are going to see that mountain move, you already believe in your heart that it is going to move before you command it to move. Too many try to command that mountain to move before they believe in their heart that it will move. Then they get frustrated when it doesn't move.

You can command that mountain to move for all eternity but if you don't believe in your heart that it's done, you are not speaking from a place of faith. You are probably in mental assent at best. The word says, "all things are possible to those who believe," not "all things are possible to those who speak." I want you to look at Mark 11 one more time. It says, "...but believes that those things he says will be done, he will have whatever he says."

Faith's confession is confessing with our mouth what we already know to be true in our heart. Romans 10:8-10 "…the word is near you, in your mouth and in your heart" (that is, the word of faith which we preach): that if you confess with your mouth and believe in your heart that God has raised Jesus from the dead, you will be saved. For with the heart one believes unto righteousness, and with the mouth confession is made unto salvation."

Look at that last verse, "For with the heart one believes…and with the mouth confession is made." Believing is first before speaking. Psalm 116:10 says, "I believed, therefore I spoke…" Matthew 12:14 says, "…For out of the abundance of the heart the mouth speaks." Many times, I have been healed before I even spoke a word. I would be in prayer sitting before the Lord in silence, meditating on the word in my heart, simply mulling over it and fellowshipping with the Holy Spirit. Allowing Him to bring light and revelation to the verse. Then I would receive the word in my heart, my mind is renewed to its truth and the power or life of the word is released. I was instantly healed.

There have been other times where I wasn't instantly healed but I knew, that I knew, that I knew it was done. It was already done in my heart. At that moment I confessed it and it wasn't long before the healing manifested. My confession was made out of a place of true faith. Out of revelation. Out of a renewed mind. I was fully convinced that what God had promised, He would bring to pass.

I think that our words would carry more weight, if we weighed our words more before we spoke them. Jesus only said what He heard the Father say, and everything Jesus said came to pass. We can learn a valuable truth here. You may say, "well that's because that was Jesus. I'm not Jesus." Yes, that's true, you are not Jesus. But let's look at another man who wasn't Jesus, who walked in this same level of faith and answered prayer.

Let us look at 1 Samuel 3:19, "So Samuel grew, and the Lord was with him and let none of his words fall to the ground" My...my...my, that's an extraordinary statement. None of his words fell to the ground. That means everything he declared came to pass. Why? We will find the answer in verse 35 of chapter 2 when God said, "...I will raise up for myself a faithful priest (Samuel) who shall do according to what is in My heart and in My mind." Why did Samuel's words all come to pass? Because he spoke what was in God's heart and what He heard God say. Faith comes by hearing and hearing the Word of God.

The word of the Lord came to Samuel and when the word came, faith came. Then Samuel spoke. You see, the word of the Lord is just as powerful coming out of your mouth as it is coming out of God's mouth. If you are fully convinced that what God has spoken will come to pass, nothing can stop it from coming to pass. How was Samuel fully convinced? How was Abraham fully convinced? How was Jesus fully convinced? Because they knew God. They knew the One who spoke it and the One who stood behind His Word.

Remember what I said at the beginning of this chapter, the foundation of faith is relationship. They took God at His word. The more time we spend with God in prayer and in the word the more faith will grow...

Trust God. He is faithful. If He has spoken it, He will bring it to pass.

6

WORSHIP

MANY THINGS HAPPEN DURING WORSHIP AND THIS WILL not be an extensive listing of those things. I want to focus in the context of healing, for the sake of staying on topic. When we begin to worship the Lord is magnified in our hearts, until we begin to see Him correctly. It causes us to take our eyes off of us and our problems, and rightly put our focus on Him. It changes the atmosphere. It creates a habitation for God. The Lord is enthroned upon the praises of His people. His kingdom comes, and His will is done, on earth as it is in heaven.

There is no sickness in heaven, so when His kingdom is in manifestation sickness cannot remain. A greater kingdom has come. We have to see the Lord correctly and I don't know of any better way than worship. When the Lord steps into the room, everything changes. I've been in many environments where during worship people began to be healed and yet no one has prayed for them. How and why? Because the Healer had entered the room. The King and His kingdom had come. It is Jesus' nature to heal. If we would just put our eyes and hearts on Him, He will do what He loves to do. Heal, strengthen, and love on His people. I promise He can do it a lot faster, and a lot more efficiently, than we can.

We enter His gates through thanksgiving and His courts with praise. He is being magnified and we are beginning to see Him rightly. When we see Him rightly, a heart of worship comes. When this Spirit of worship comes, we enter into this deeper place of knowing the Lord. An honor, reverence, and fear of the Lord overtakes our hearts. Our love, our heart and our spirit begin to be poured out at His feet. We become conscious of His holiness, beauty, and nearness. Everything fades and all we are aware of is Him. He begins to fill the temple. Every cell of our being and every square inch of the room comes alive to Him.

And then Glory! His presence and His kingdom overtake everything. Jesus is light and life. Repentance comes to some as His light hits every dark area of their lives. Healing comes and sick people begin to get well. Life begins to flow into their bodies, causing dead things to come alive. This is a very special place. It is holy ground. He becomes the very air in the room. This is the place we should seek to get to in every service. God takes center stage and He doesn't need our help. If we continue to minister to the Lord, keeping our hearts and eyes fixed on Him in worship, He will do in a few moments what would take us days, months, or even years to do.

This doesn't only take place in corporate settings though. In fact, it should happen more often in the secret place. I can't count how many times I've been healed in my room on my knees worshiping the Lord. I don't go into it saying, let me go worship the Lord so He will heal my body. I do it because I love Him. He's so good and my natural response is to worship Him. When I get to that still place, where all I am aware of is Him. His divinity touches my humanity, and resurrection life begins to flow, making me whole spirit, soul, and body.

Another scripture that has meant a lot to me along the lines of praise and worship is Isaiah 61:3 "...To give them beauty for ashes, The oil of joy for mourning, The garment of praise for the spirit of heaviness." The garment of praise! There have been times through the years where I have been down and feeling really heavy from anxiety, depression, or some type of sickness attacking my body.

I remember the first time I came across the power of this scripture years ago. I was sitting at my dining room table trying to study the word but I just couldn't shake this heavy feeling of depression trying to come on me because of this sickness I had been battling for a while without getting any results. I had just about reached my limit when I came across this scripture. I sat there saying it over and over again. Praise for heaviness...praise for heaviness. I then stood up and walked into the living room and began to praise God with everything that was in me.

After about fifteen minutes of this, this energy and joy hit me and the whole atmosphere around me changed. I was overwhelmed with joy and thankfulness to the Lord. I felt so happy and light and every bit of heaviness was gone. I felt absolutely refreshed. I have had many similar experiences concerning praise. We are supposed to be a joyful people. Walking around looking somber and repressed doesn't make us more spiritual or humble.

As Christians, our natural disposition should be joy and peace. If this isn't the case, then we need to seek the Lord to find out what's off. Joy and peace should be our state of being even when going through trials or carrying a burden of the Lord. Remember Jesus said, "My yoke is easy and my burden is light." Jesus, who went through more than any other man and had to carry the heaviest burden anyone has ever had to carry, was a peaceful and joyful man.

Hebrews 1:9 "You have loved righteousness and hated lawlessness; Therefore God, Your God, has anointed You with the oil of gladness more than Your companions."

Proverbs 17: "A merry heart does good like medicine..."

7

IN THE NAME OF JESUS

There is power in the name of Jesus. There is authority in the name of Jesus. There is life in the name of Jesus. There is just something about that name. In this chapter I want to cover *authority*. We have to understand authority in order to walk in it. We have to know that it is in His name and by His authority that we can do anything. The next couple chapters are going to be about prayer and ministering healing, so I wanted to lay the foundation for how any of us can stand and command anything to leave someone's body.

Understanding this chapter will actually help you receive answers to prayer in other areas as well. First, I want to discuss what it means to come, or to do something in someone's name. Coming in someone's name means you are there for their best interest. For their glory and not your own. If you were there seeking glory for yourself, you would actually be there in your own name. For your benefit and not theirs.

John 7:18 "He who speaks from himself seeks his own glory; but He who seeks the glory of the One who sent Him is true, and there is no unrighteousness in Him." Jesus carried the Father's authority because He was there on His Father's behalf. For His Father's will and His glory. If we want to walk in Jesus' authority, we have to be there on His behalf. We are there as His representative and ambassador. Doing what He would do if He was standing there.

If I go somewhere *in someone's name*, the words that I speak are as if they were spoken by the one who sent me. Let us look at what Jesus said in John 12:49-50, "For I have not spoken on my own authority; but the Father who sent Me gave Me a command, what I should say and what I should speak. And I know that His command is everlasting life. Therefore, whatever I speak, just as the Father has told Me, so I speak."

Always remember this, the level of authority that you walk in will be in direct proportion to the level of your submission to Jesus. Authority comes down from the head. Jesus has all authority.

> Matthew 28:18, "And Jesus came and spoke to them, saying, all authority has been given to Me in heaven and on earth."

This is wonderful news. This means when we come into any situation in His name, we have all of the authority of heaven and earth backing us. If we are there to accomplish His will, the very throne of God is backing us. Remember from chapter one, it is His will to heal.

> Luke 9:1-2, "Then He called His twelve disciples together and gave them power and authority over all demons, and to cure diseases. He sent them to preach the kingdom of God and to heal the sick."

What is it about the name of Jesus? Why is there so much authority and power in His name. Well, let's look and see. We will find our answer in Philippians 2:5-11, "...Jesus Christ, who, being in the form of God, did not consider it robbery to be equal with God, but made Himself of no reputation, taking on the form of a bond servant, and coming in the likeness of men. And being found in the appearance as a man, He humbled Himself and became obedient to the point of death, even the death of the Cross. Therefore, God also highly exalted Him and has given Him the name which is above every name, that at the name of Jesus every knee should bow, of those in heaven, and of those on the earth, and of those under the earth, and that every tongue should confess that Jesus Christ is Lord, to the glory of the Father."

Why is there so much power in His name? Because, it is the name of the victorious, triumphant, King of Kings and Lord of Lords. Because of Jesus' obedience to the Father, because of His humility, the Father has given Him the name above every other name. That's why we use the name of Jesus! Because it is above every other name.

Cancer is a name, heart disease is a name, diabetes is a name, dementia is a name, hepatitis is a name. And every single one of these must bow to the name of Jesus. Jesus is Lord over all of these. He is Lord over every sickness and disease. And Jesus has given us His authority and His name to use. In John chapter 14, verses 12-14, Jesus said, "Most assuredly, I say to you, he who believes in Me, the works that I do and greater works than these he will do, because I go to My Father. And whatever you ask in My name, that I will do, that the Father may be glorified in the Son. If you ask anything in my name, I will do it."

This is extraordinary. Greater works we will do. Jesus gave us His name to use and then He is seated at the right hand of the Father in the place of complete authority and power, bringing to pass what we ask for in His name. We have to have faith in Jesus and we have to have faith in His name. It's only in His name that we stand. Peter knew this. Let us look at what he told the people when the lame man was healed who was at the gate of the temple which is called beautiful.

> Acts 3:12-13, 16, "So when Peter saw it, he responded to the people: Men of Israel, why do you marvel at this? Or why look so intently at us, as though by our power or godliness we had made this man walk? The God of Abraham, Isaac, and Jacob, the God of our fathers, glorified His Servant Jesus... And His name, and faith in His name, has made this man strong, whom you see and know. Yes, the faith which comes through Him has given him this perfect soundness in the presence of you all."

Jesus is a king. Being a king, He has a kingdom. His kingdom is above and far superior to every other kingdom. In Jesus' kingdom, His perfect will is being done. In the Lord's prayer Jesus told His disciples to pray your kingdom come, Your will be done, on earth as in heaven. In heaven everything is in alignment with the Lordship of Jesus and His perfect will. When we were born again, we were delivered from the kingdom of darkness and translated into the Lord's kingdom.

This means that we are no longer under the dominion of Satan or the things of this world. We are not limited to the natural as we are citizens of a supernatural kingdom. What overcomes the people of this world, does not overcome us. We are not at the mercy of the limited knowledge and understanding of man. The doctors may tell you that you only have one month to live. Thankfully you are not bound to that fate as you are a supernatural being, who is a citizen of a supernatural kingdom, which is ruled by a supernatural God. One who heals His people. Let us look at the superiority of King Jesus and His kingdom.

Ephesians 1:20-22 says, "...Which He worked in Christ when He raised Him from the dead and seated Him at His right hand in heavenly places, far above all principality and power and might and dominion, and every name that is named, not only in this age but also in that which is to come. And He has put all things under His feet, and gave Him to be head over all things to the church." He put all things under His feet! All things! All things! All things! When we truly know that all things are under Jesus' feet, we will begin to see that all things are under our feet, as we are His body.

If we go a little deeper into Ephesians, we will see this truth. Eph 2:4-6 "But God who is rich in mercy, because of His great love with which He loved us, even when we were dead in trespasses, made us alive together with Christ, and raised us to sit together in the heavenly places in Christ Jesus." We too are above all things and have authority over Satan's kingdom. Sickness, disease, poverty, hopelessness, and fear are a part of his kingdom. Demons are a part of his kingdom. Sometimes demons are involved in someone's sickness. In that instance, we need to deal with the demon before their bodies can be healed.

This is nothing to be afraid of or intimidated by. Demons are already defeated. You don't have to fight some battle with them. You just invoke the victory that Jesus has already won. He has already defeated Satan, every demon, death, hell, and the grave. We stand before them in His victory and in His authority. We are basically evicting them from someone's body. In the name of Jesus, they have to go. There's no questions about it. Jesus has all authority, which means they have none. Don't worry, you are not doing this by any power that you possess. You are doing it in the power of the Holy Spirit. Greater is He who is in you than he who is in the world. You command and the Holy Spirit executes.

I love what Jesus told His disciples in Luke 10:18-19, "…I saw Satan fall like lightning from heaven. Behold, I give you authority to trample upon serpents and scorpions, and over all the power of the enemy, and nothing shall by any means hurt you." We are not to be impressed or frightened by anything the enemy is doing. He is full of lies, and deceit. He has no authority. He will try and make you believe he does through intimidation and fear. If you feel fear trying to creep in, you slap it down with the shield of faith. Then you slide that sharp sword of the Spirit, the Word of God, in his chest as you stomp on his head putting him in his place.

I have no time for the devil. Don't go around demon hunting. If they get in the way, deal with them, but spend your time looking at Jesus and fellowshipping with Him. He is so much more beautiful to look at and fun to hang out with. That and not all sickness has a demon behind it. Actually, the majority of them don't, but you do need to know how to deal with them when they are.

Mark 16:17-18 "And these signs shall follow them that believe: In My name they will cast out demons; they will speak with new tongues; they will take up serpents; and if they drink anything deadly, it will be no means hurt them; they will lay hands on the sick and they will recover."

8

BAPTISM OF THE HOLY SPIRIT

ONE OF THE MOST IMPORTANT ACTS FOR A CHRISTIAN to partake in, apart from the new birth and baptism in water, is the baptism of the Holy Spirit. It is within this baptism that the Christian is clothed with the Holy Spirit and power to be a witness unto Christ. To work the works seen in the ministry of Jesus, we need the baptism of the Holy Spirit. We have to remember that Jesus did everything as a man clothed with the Holy Spirit. This is very exciting and brings much hope and faith, that we too can walk as Jesus walked, doing the works of the Father.

If we are going to pray for the sick, and win the lost, we need the power of the Holy Spirit. The Holy Spirit is within us, for us, and He is upon us for others. Every born-again child of God has the Holy

Spirit living on the inside of them. This takes place at the new birth when we are born again, but there is a separate infilling that takes place after the new birth. We need to seek the Lord for this baptism. He is the one who has promised the Holy Spirit and He is actually the One who baptizes us.

> Luke 24-49: "...Thus it is written, and thus it was necessary for the Christ to suffer and to rise from the dead the third day, and that repentance and remission of sins should be preached in His name to all nations, beginning at Jerusalem. And you are witnesses of these things. Behold, I send the promise of the Father upon you; but tarry in the city of Jerusalem until you are endued with power from on high."

> Acts 1:8 "But you should receive power when the Holy Spirit has come upon you; and you shall be witnesses to Me in Jerusalem, and in all Judea and Samaria, and to the end of the earth."

> John 1:33-34 "...He who sent me to baptize with water said to me, 'Upon whom you see the Spirit descending and remaining on Him, this is He who baptizes with the Holy Spirit' and I have seen and testified that this is the Son of God."

In the word it says that we will receive power to be witnesses when the Holy Spirit comes upon us. What is a witness...and a witness unto what? A witness is someone who has seen, can prove, validate or attest to something being true. Someone who has knowledge of an event or change from personal observation or experience. Someone who can testify to something or someone with evidence to their claim. We are to be witnesses of Jesus. We are supposed to witness to the truth that He is the Son of God. We are supposed to reveal Him to people.

Revealing the works that He has done and that He still is doing. We are supposed to witness to the fact that He has overcome sin and sickness and that He wants to set others free from these things. We are supposed to witness the fact that He died for their sins and has been raised to life again. That He is alive and sitting at the right hand of God. That He is King and that His kingdom is superior to the kingdom of darkness and the kingdoms of this world. A witness to the unconditional love which He longs to express towards His children.

In Proverbs 14:25 it says, "A true witness delivers souls." Delivers souls from what? From the same things that your life was delivered from. Delivers souls from sin, depression, anxiety, addiction, sickness and disease, poverty, the works of darkness. In order to do this, we are going to need power and this is what the Baptism of the Holy Spirit is for. We need the Holy Spirit! We cannot do these things in any natural power that we possess on our own. We need the same power of God that Jesus walked in when He was on the earth.

> Acts 10:38 "how God anointed Jesus of Nazareth with the Holy Spirit and power, who went about doing good and healing all who were oppressed by the devil, for God was with Him."

> Luke 4:18 "The Spirit of the Lord is upon Me, because He has anointed Me to preach the gospel to the poor; He has sent Me to heal the broken hearted, to proclaim liberty to the captives and recovery of sight to the blind, to set at liberty all who are oppressed; to proclaim the acceptable year of the Lord."

Here we see how a man filled with the Holy Spirit is supposed to walk. Jesus is our perfect example. We are supposed to follow Him.

> John 14:12 "he who believes in Me, the works that I do he will do also; and greater works than these will he do because I go to the Father."

The Holy Spirit is a promised gift from God, and as with all gifts from God, it is meant to be received by faith. It wasn't meant to be strived for or begged for but asked for and received.

> Luke 11:11-13 "So I say to you, ask, and it will be given to you; seek, and you will find; knock, and it will be opened to you. For everyone who asks receives and he who seeks finds, and to him who knocks it will be opened. If a son asks for bread from any father among you, will he give him a stone? Or if he asks for a fish will he give him a serpent instead of a fish? If you then, being evil, know how to give good gifts to your children, how much more will your heavenly Father give the Holy Spirit to them that ask Him!"

Everyone who asks receives. The Father is more than willing to give us the Holy Spirit.

When the woman with the issue of blood was healed by touching the hem of Jesus' garment, His garment wasn't made of some special type of material or something. It was the anointing of the Holy Spirit upon Him. The same when Peter's shadow was healing people along the side of the road. There was no power in his shadow to heal, it was the Holy Spirit who was overshadowing him that healed the people. I remember one time the Lord told me, "The hem of My garment, is the hem of your garment." If we want to walk in the footsteps of Jesus, casting out demons, healing the sick, and raising the dead, we need to be clothed in the power and presence of the Holy Spirit.

9

PRAYER

IF YOU NOTICED, NONE OF THE CHAPTERS PROCEEDING this one, have been about getting people to pray for you to be healed. I first wanted to open your eyes to other ways. You may not always have someone there to pray for you. If you never grow and always depend upon the prayers of others, there is a revelation and an intimacy with the Lord that you are missing out on.

The Lord loves all of His children and wills that all should come to Him in faith believing He wants to answer their prayers and heal their bodies. I remember what Jesus told His disciples when He was getting ready to leave, because the cross was soon approaching and He was going back to the Father.

John 16:23-24, 26-27 "And in that day you will ask Me nothing. Most assuredly, I say to you, whatever you ask the Father in My name He will give you. Until now you have asked nothing in My name. Ask, and you will receive, that your joy may be full... In that day you will ask in My name, and I do not say to you that I shall pray the Father for you; for the Father Himself loves you, because you have loved Me, and have believed that I came forth from God."

A disciple is a student. We will never stop being students as the Lord is always teaching us something. The vastness of His wisdom is limitless. Though as we grow in our relationship with Him and are taught by Him there comes a point where we need to start stepping out there in faith doing what He has taught us to do. That, and we need to mature so we can pray for younger believers or the lost.

With that said though, don't condemn yourself or stop going to others for prayer if you need to. Jesus always met people where their faith was. If you haven't reached that place of maturity of faith concerning a certain area, by all means get with a brother or sister in the faith that is strong in that area. We are a body of believers. We are meant to stand together. There is power in numbers. The word says that one can put a thousand to flight and two 10,000. There is also the prayer of agreement. Matthew 18:19, "Again I say to you that If two of you agree on earth concerning anything that they ask, it will be done for them by My Father in heaven."

Let us now cover prayer. Because this is a book about healing, I will stay along that same track when talking about prayer. If this was a book about prayer, I would go a lot deeper about the different forms of prayer, about intimacy, the Spirit of Prayer, waiting on the Lord, and becoming one with the Lord through the communion of prayer. I would love to go into them, but let us stay on topic. Even within the context of praying for healing there are many different types of prayer. Before going into them let me establish the fact that we are supposed to be praying for the sick.

As I stated in the last chapter, Mark 16 tells us that signs will follow those who believe. Then it goes into talking about believers laying hands on the sick and them recovering. We are also commissioned to heal the sick in Matthew 18:7-8, "And as you go, preach, saying, 'The kingdom of heaven is at hand.' Heal the sick, cleanse the lepers, raise the dead, cast out demons. Freely you have received, freely give."

Jesus healed the sick. Then His disciples after Him healed the sick. So, we too are to heal the sick. Now concerning the different types of prayer for doing this. I have personally seen people healed by everything from commanding prayer (telling a sickness, pain, or condition to get out of someone's body), to asking God to remove a sickness from someone's body, to falling on the mercy of God and just saying "Jesus Help," or at times just saying the name of Jesus over and over again.

I've known people to not even say a word, but to just hug a person and have them be healed. Their tears were the prayer. When determining which form of prayer to use, I usually go with my heart or what I'm feeling in the spirit in the moment. We want to be Spirit led. I go with where my conviction or my compassion is. Very often Jesus was moved with compassion when praying for the sick. We also see that Jesus very seldom healed anyone the same way. He said that He only said what He heard the Father saying and He only did what He saw the Father doing. We want to be this same way.

If you have the time don't be too quick to pray. Hear what the Lord wants you to do. The way He wants to heal someone this time may not be the same way that He healed someone last time. We would be a lot more effective and see more people healed if we did this. Now I understand there are times in emergency situations where we need to pray immediately. The Lord very mercifully meets us in these moments with His power.

Let us go with commanding prayer first. We saw in previous chapters that authority has been given to us over sickness and disease. This means that we can approach a person who is sick and with their permission, exercise authority over what is ailing their body. If it is cancer, we command that cancer to get out of their body. If it is pain, we command that pain to leave. If it is a broken bone, we command that bone to mend and be made whole.

You may wonder, why do we command the sickness to leave? To understand this, we must know what Jesus gave us when He gave us authority over sickness and disease. The word authority means - the power or the right to give orders, make decisions and enforce obedience. We see an example of this in the interaction between Jesus and the centurion in Matthew chapter 8. Let's take a look at that account.

Matthew 8: 8-10 "The centurion answered and said, Lord I am not worthy that You should come under my roof. But only speak the word and my servant will be healed. For I also am a man under authority, having soldiers under me. And I say to this one, 'Go, and he goes; and to another, 'Come,' and he comes; and to my servant, 'Do this,' and he does it. When Jesus heard it, He marveled, and said to those who follow, "Assuredly, I say to you, I have not found such great faith, not even in Israel!"

It was accredited to this guy that he had great faith, because of his understanding of the authority that Jesus carried. He was a man of authority. The centurion knew, if he made a command to someone or something under his authority that it had to obey. His soldiers were under His authority, the same way sickness is under our authority. Sickness was not in God's original design for someone's body, so we have the authority and the right to command it to leave.

Luke 9:1 "Then Jesus called His twelve disciples together and gave them power and authority over demons and to cure diseases."

When praying for others you will need to get their permission to exercise this authority over their body. They have to want to be healed. We don't have authority over the will of others. I have asked people to pray for them and they told me "no". At this point my hands were tied. I can walk off and pray that the Lord have mercy on them and heal them, but as far as taking authority over the situation, I can't. They have chosen to keep the thing. Now if I'm praying for myself or my child, then I have the ability to exercise authority. That, and If the person you are praying for is unconscious. In that situation the person doesn't have the ability to give you permission. Before going to the next type of prayer, I want to point out that the majority of all the prayers that Jesus prayed concerning healing or demons were commands.

Next, we have petition prayers. This is where we ask God to heal someone's body. We can have confidence in our prayers to God for healing. It is God's will to heal; we know this. One of my favorite scriptures for this type of prayer is 1 John 5:14-15, "Now this is the confidence that we have in Him, that if we ask anything according to His will, He hears us. And if we know that He hears us, whatever we ask, we know that we have the petitions that we have asked of Him." Trust me, God wants the person you're praying for healed more than you want them healed. Many times, I've asked God to heal someone's body and God has wonderfully healed them. It's His nature to heal.

Next, we have what I would like to call 911 prayers. This is where you don't have time or even the words to pray. You just throw yourself on the mercy of God and say, "Help!" I remember one time in particular when I was very close to the point of death and right before I knew that I was about to go, I whispered "Jesus help." That's all I got out and the power of God hit me and I was completely healed.

> Psalm 107:19-20, "Lord, Help! They cried in their trouble, and He saved them from their distress. He sent out His word and healed them, snatching them from the door of death." NLT

As you see there are many different ways to pray for the sick, but this isn't an exhaustive list by any means. Have faith and courage. Be led by the Holy Spirit and you will see many healed and restored to health. Whether someone is healed instantly or over time varies. We see this in the life of Jesus. Many were healed instantly, but when He prayed for the ten lepers it says that they were healed along the way. It is always great to see someone instantly healed, but never be discouraged if they're not. Our part is to pray, it is the Lord's part to heal.

If you pray for someone and you don't see an immediate change, stand in faith believing that the Lord will bring it to pass. Many times, when praying for someone, I didn't see any change, but as they went home and went to sleep that night, they woke up the next day completely healed. We do want to have an expectation though to see people healed on the spot. After you pray for someone, ask them to try and do something that they couldn't do before. If you were praying about knee pain. Have them stand up and squat or bend so they can put pressure on the knee. If the pain is still there, pray again. After praying, have them try it again.

A lot of times people are healed in the action. If there is no change, pray again. You may say, "How many times do I pray?" I usually pray three times or so, but I have known people to pray 6 or 7 times and the person be healed on the 7th time. There is no formula or anything. I always pray as long as the person wants prayer. If you can tell the person is becoming uncomfortable then bless them and encourage them letting them know that sometimes people are healed over time.

Before moving on to the next chapter, I want to bring up the laying on of hands. We don't always have to lay hands on someone to pray for them to be healed. Many times, Jesus just pronounced healing over someone and they were healed. At the same time, we can't overlook the power of laying hands on someone. Mark 16 said they will lay hands on the sick and they will recover. When Jesus entered Peter's mother in law's house, it says that He laid His hand on her and the fever left her.

Also, when Jesus came down from the mountain in Matthew 8, it says that He put out His hand and touched the leper and He was healed. Habakkuk 3:3-4 says, "...His glory covered the heavens, And the earth was full of His praise. His brightness was like the light; He had rays flashing from His hand, and there His power was hidden." There is a transference through the laying on of hands. We see it throughout the entire Bible. The blessing was passed down from generation to generation through the laying on of hands.

We see this when Isaac laid his hand on Jacob and then at the end of Jacob's life, he laid his hand on his children. The priests used to lay their hand on the offering before they sacrificed it. Spiritual gifts are imparted through the laying on of hands. We see this when Paul told Timothy not to forget the gift that was imparted to him through the laying on of hands. The Holy Spirit was received through the laying on of hands. Wisdom was imparted through the laying on of hands. This is seen when Moses laid his hand on Joshua. The elders laid their hands on someone when commissioning them and sending them off.

Why the hand? I want you to notice that every one of these was done by a person in a position of authority. The hand in the Bible represents many different things, especially the right hand. It represents position, power, strength, and authority.

Psalm 89:13 "You have a mighty arm; Strong is Your hand, and high is Your right hand."

Exodus 15:6 "Your right hand, O Lord, has become glorious in power; Your right hand, O Lord, has dashed the enemy in pieces."

Luke 22:69 "Hereafter the Son of Man will sit on the right hand of the power of God."

1 Peter 3:22 "Who has gone into heaven and is at the right hand of God, angels and authorities and powers having been made subject to Him."

Isaiah 48:13 "Indeed My hand has laid the foundation of the earth, And My right hand has stretched out the heavens..."

With the hand also, it is the place that you wear a ring. Rings stand for a lot. In the story of the prodigal son, the Father put a ring on His son's finger upon his return. This ring signified sonship. Then we have the story of Esther. The King gave Mordecai his signet ring.

Then he said in Esther 8:8, "You yourselves write a decree concerning the Jews, as you please, in the King's name, and seal it with the King's ring; for whatever is written in the King's name and sealed with the King's signet ring no one can revoke." We also see this when Pharaoh gave Joseph his signet ring, setting him over all the land of Egypt and telling him, "...without your consent no man may lift his hand or foot in all the land of Egypt."

The ring is also significant in the covenant of marriage. When God gave us Jesus, He gave us all of these. Let us look at Haggai 2:22-23, "And I will (in the distant future) overthrow the throne of kingdoms and I will destroy the strength of the kingdoms of the (ungodly) nations... In that day, says the Lord of hosts, will I take you, O Zerubbabel, My servant, the son of Shealtiel, says the Lord, and will make you (through the Messiah, your descendant) My signet ring; for I have chosen you (as the one with whom to renew My covenant to David's line), says the Lord of hosts."

We see here that Jesus is God's signet ring which He has given to us. In Jesus we have sonship, authority, and covenant. When we lay hands on people, we are standing there as a covenant child of God, in the place of His authority releasing His blessing over their body. I'm sure there are other significant things that take place when we are laying hands on people. It is a point of contact, which gives people a moment that encourages them to release their faith. It could also be that when we lay hands on people, we are releasing life from our spirit into their body.

If I get a chance to lay my hand on someone when I pray for them, I do it. But if I am unable to lay hands on them, I'm not affected by it or anything. I still pray with the same level of faith and authority. Some get caught up thinking they always have to lay their hand on somebody for their prayer to be effective. It just isn't so. I've known many to be healed from praying over the phone or just standing next to someone and praying. Jesus healed many with a simple word; "Arise."

James 5:16 "...The effective fervent prayer of a righteous man avails much."

10

WORDS OF KNOWLEDGE

There are several gifts of the Spirit in connection to healing. These gifts are in 1 Corinthians 12. The word says that these gifts are given for the profit of all. It also says in the 11th verse of chapter 12, that it is the same Spirit who works all these, and He distributes them to each one individually as He wills. The Word of Knowledge is one of these gifts. A word of knowledge is very powerful and effective in ministering and evangelizing. But what are words of knowledge?

A word of knowledge is when previously unknown information is conveyed by the Holy Spirit about someone. This could be about a person's past or their present. It is a divine revelation. The range of information given could be vast. It could be about anything from a disease they have or something in their past that means something to them. When the Holy Spirit reveals something about their past it is usually to bring the person into the realization that God is real. And not only is He real, but He knows me and He sees me. This usually sparks hope and faith in their heart to receive from the Lord what He wants to give to them. Whether that is healing in their body or a prophetic word depends on what the Lord is doing in the moment. An example of this is when Jesus was with the woman at the well. Let's look at this account.

> John 4:16-18 "Jesus said to her, "Go, call your husband, and come here." The woman answered and said, "I have no husband." Jesus said to her, "You have well said, 'I have no husband,' for you have had five husbands, and the one whom you now have is not your husband; in that you spoke truly."

How did Jesus know these things? You may say, because He is Jesus and He knows all things. We have to remember that in the book Philippians it says that Jesus made Himself of no reputation taking on the form of a man. In the New Living Translation, it says "He gave up His divine privileges; He took the humble position of a slave and was born as a human being. When He appeared in human form." Jesus never stopped being God, but for a season and for His assignment on earth He gave up His divine privileges. He needed to do this because what was lost in the garden by a man named Adam, had to be gained back by a man.

We have to understand, as I stated earlier in this book, that Jesus did everything before the Cross as a man filled with the Holy Spirit. In the same way, we are children of God filled with the Holy Spirit. After Jesus revealed this information to the woman, information no one would know but God, it sparked faith in her and she ran back to her hometown and told everyone, "Come, see a Man who told me all things that I ever did. Could this be the Christ?" Just one word of knowledge sparked faith in a woman's heart that led to a revival and a city coming to the Lord. Do you see the power of a word of knowledge?

Now let's talk about where they come in concerning healing. If I'm on the street ministering to people and the Holy Spirit gives me the word *arthritis*. When I ask the person in front of me if they have arthritis, they're going to wonder how could I possibly know that about them. This is going to cause them to let their guard down and birth a hope in their heart that when I tell them God wants to heal them when I pray for them, they allow me to pray.

I then pray, and more often than not, the Lord heals the person of that condition. The grace or the power of God for the healing is released in the word of the Lord. The Lord sent His word and healed them. A word of knowledge for healing is basically God saying, "I want to heal this condition right now." We just need to learn to partner with God. We were never meant to do this alone. We couldn't do this alone. This is still Jesus' ministry. He has just allowed us into His works. Anything outside of partnership with the Holy Spirit is a work of the flesh. We need to learn to listen to two people at the same time. The person standing in front of us and the Holy Spirit. A word of knowledge is very effective and really connects people to the voice and heart of God in the moment.

A word of knowledge can come in several different ways. It could be that still small voice of the Holy Spirit. It can be a picture in your spirit that you see. You may see a kidney or a heart or something. It can be just an impression or a knowing. You just know the information about them. It can be a quick vision of something. I have actually had a dream the day before meeting someone, and in the dream I was given knowledge about them.

Sometimes you can see in the spirit and see either an angel highlighting something or I have known people to see words written in the spirit over someone's head. It could be a pain that you are experiencing in your body that isn't yours. If you walk up to someone and all of a sudden you have a pain in a certain area of your body that you didn't have before. It could be a word of knowledge that the person you are talking to, or someone near you, is experiencing pain in that area. There are many ways the Lord speaks to us. We just need to be open to the different ways, and to have an expectation that He will.

11

WORD OF WISDOM/ACTS OF OBEDIENCE

ANOTHER GIFT OF THE HOLY SPIRIT IS THE WORD OF Wisdom. These are similar to a Word of Knowledge, in the fact that they are revelatory gifts, but different in operation. The word of wisdom is divine revelation and insight on the solution to an obstacle or problem. This could range anywhere from an invention that changes the effectiveness of how something works, to the cure for a disease. The Lord is all-knowing and has an answer to every problem that ever existed. He is wisdom.

Words of wisdom can come in the same way that words of knowledge come. Some ways are dreams, visions, a still small voice, an impression or knowing, or through other people. I tied acts of obedience into this chapter because when we receive revelation concerning something, we will need to act on what is revealed for the intended result to come. James 1:5-7 says, "If any of you lacks wisdom, let him ask of God, who gives to all liberally without reproach, and it will be given to him. But let him ask in faith, with no doubting, for he who doubts is like a wave of the sea driven and tossed by the wind. For let not that man suppose that he will receive anything from the Lord; he is a double minded man and unstable in all his ways."

This is basically saying, when God gives you the wisdom you asked for, don't doubt and not act on what He told you. If you do, you will not receive what that wisdom is intended to produce. I remember a funny example of this, but a perfect one. A couple years ago, I developed toenail fungus on some of my toenails. One night during this I had a dream. In the dream an older man walked up to me, I knew the man to represent wisdom. He looked at me and said, "You know... tea tree oil will get rid of that toenail fungus." That's all he said and then I woke up.

I went and bought some tea tree oil and began to use it on my toenails. Over time my toenails improved tremendously. I later found out through Google that

that was a thing. So, you see, I had a choice to make. I could have either brushed off the wisdom revealed, or I could obey what was revealed and get the intended results.

There are many similar examples to this in the Bible. There was that one time when Jesus told the ten lepers to go show themselves unto the priests. It says that they were healed along the way. There was also the time when He healed the blind man by putting mud on his eyes. He then told him to go and wash in the pool of Siloam. It says that he went and washed and came back seeing. There was also the story of the leper Naaman. Let's go over this one.

The story takes place in 2 Kings 5. In this story Naaman, a commander of the army of Syria, had leprosy. He was told that he should go see the prophet Elisha. When Naaman got to Elisha, Elisha told him to go wash in the Jordan river seven times and he would be healed. Naaman had a decision to make in that moment. He could either reject the word of wisdom or he could obey it.

Initially he rejected it and refused to obey the instructions. Then one of his servants convinced him to do it. It says that he went and washed and was made clean. He obeyed the word of wisdom and was healed. He then replied, now I know there is no other God in all the earth, besides the God of Israel. Words of wisdom are very powerful. When they truly come from the Lord and are acted on, they always bring the intended result. There is one thing I want to touch on concerning acts of obedience. Make sure the Lord is telling you to do something. Don't try to do something to make something happen when the Lord didn't tell you to do it. That could be considered tempting the Lord. Like when Satan tempted Jesus in the wilderness and told Him to jump off the pinnacle of the temple. Basically, he said, "Jump the angels will catch you." Jesus replied, "It has been said, 'You shall not tempt the Lord your God.'"

Some people jump off the cliff, supposedly in the name of faith, hoping God will catch them. Did God tell you to jump? If He did, great; jump! I've known some people who threw away their medicine and said, "I'm standing in faith I'm healed." Only to be discouraged a few days later when they had to start taking their medicine again. This is doing more harm to your faith then good.

I've also known some whom God told them to stop taking their medicine because they were healed. And sure enough, when they stopped taking their medicine, they never had to take it again because they were healed. Faith isn't just stepping out there into the unknown hoping something is there. Faith is stepping out onto something more solid and dependable then the ground underneath your feet. It's stepping out onto the Word of God.

HOW TO KEEP YOUR HEALING

THIS CHAPTER, TO BE HONEST, IS A CHAPTER THAT I wish I would have read a long time ago. It would have prevented many discouraging moments and battles that had to be fought over and over again. We have an enemy who does not want us to be healed and healthy. Sometimes after getting a breakthrough in a certain area or healing, he will try to bring that very same condition back on you. Over the years I have often had to fight battles after winning a battle.

Sometimes there are two battles. One to get free, and then one to stay free. I didn't know this initially, and on several occasions, I lost a healing. For example, if my knee was healed of pain, a few days later that pain would hit that same spot in my knee. Often-times this is the enemy trying to get you to doubt that you were ever healed to begin with. When that pain comes back in that same area, I have a decision to make. To rebuke that pain, telling it to leave because I was healed and will not let it come back. Or I can allow doubt to enter my mind and accept it back into my body, thinking, 'I guess I wasn't healed'. This is a real thing, I promise you. It doesn't happen every time you receive a healing, but the Devil will try you in this area. That's why you have to have a firm foundation in the Word of God and the truths revealed in the different chapters of this book.

We have to have our shield of faith up and the Word of God in our mouths. We are to resist those symptoms the same way that we resist temptation. Because it is in fact a temptation. A temptation to doubt what the Lord has done in your body. It is an easy battle to win once you are aware of what is going on and stand against it. It may not seem like it, but just hold your ground in faith standing on the word. I like what Randy Clark used to say. He would say, "the symptoms are not the sickness." I love that! It's so true.

If I have been healed of something and a symptom tries to come back upon me, I see it as a lie. A phantom deception of the enemy trying to get me to come into agreement with his lie, so he can steal from me. I've fallen for his trick before, but no more.

I desire to save you from falling into his trap. One way to really stand strong and keep all God has done in your life is *thanksgiving and praise.* This is a big one. Faith thrives in a heart of praise. I am always reminded of the story of Abraham, which we have already mentioned in this book. I will mention it again here, as it is relevant.

Romans 4:19-20, "And not being weak in faith, he did not consider his own body, already as good as dead (since he was about a hundred years old), and the deadness of Sarah's womb. He did not waver at the promise of God through unbelief, but was strengthened in faith giving glory to God." That's it. He did not consider his own body (symptoms), but was strengthened in faith, giving glory to God. Want to stay strong and keep your healing, keep your faith up and your heart on God in praise.

A thankful heart is precious and keeps our eyes on Jesus. Jesus saves to the uttermost. Proverbs 10:22 "The blessing of the Lord makes one rich, And He adds no sorrow with it." When the Lord does something, He does it completely. He doesn't bless us and then take it back. He doesn't heal us and then say 'they don't deserve that I'm taking it back.' We aren't healed on our own merit anyway. It's by His grace and mercy and the finished work of Christ. It's on Jesus' merit that we receive anything from God. This is a good thing though. It means we are always in position and in right standing to receive from God. The Lord is good. This is a foundational truth that we can never allow to waver.

We must know that He is good, and He is good all the time. When the Lord heals our bodies, it is ours, and if something tries to steal that from you, you resist it. The word says, "resist the Devil and he will flee." Stand your ground my brothers and sisters. Fight the good fight of faith. I pray that nothing given to you from the Lord is ever lost. I declare over you Nahum 1:9, "...Affliction will not rise up a second time."

TESTIMONIES

REVELATION 19:9-10 "THEN HE SAID TO ME, 'WRITE: blessed are those who are called to the marriage supper of the Lamb!' And he said to me, 'These are true sayings of God.' And I fell at his feet to worship him. But he said to me, 'see that you do not do that! I am your fellow servant, and of your brethren who have the testimony of Jesus. Worship God! For the testimony of Jesus is the spirit of prophecy.'

This last chapter I wanted to give testimonies of the healing power of God. It says here that the testimony of Jesus is the spirit of prophecy. This means every testimony I give is an invitation, or prophecy, for God to do it again. Even if I don't give a testimony concerning the exact thing that you are suffering from, I am still testifying of Jesus being the healer. You can allow that to build faith in your heart and receive healing from Jesus who heals all who come to Him.

One year while I was at work, I had a coworker come up to me and tell me that she was leaving the company. I asked her why and she told me that she had brain cancer. I remember going back to my office for a little while as I sat at my desk thinking over this. Then all of a sudden, this sense of injustice rose up in me. I then walked up to the young lady and told her, "I'm going to pray for you and Jesus is going to heal you."

Right there in the middle of the store with customers walking around us, I commanded that cancer to get out of her body in the name of Jesus. I then told her to continue to thank Jesus for her healing and to not listen to, or get away from, people talking unbelief. I saw this girl a couple months later, who had only been given months to live by the doctors. I almost didn't recognize her, as she had put on weight and looked healthy. When she saw me, she ran up to me and told me that she needed to tell me something. She then told me, "I am cancer free!" She said that she just kept thanking God for her healing after we prayed and the cancer left.

Another time while I was at work, I walked into the breakroom and a coworker was having a heart attack. I immediately walked around the table and started to command it to stop and for him to be healed in the name of Jesus. He stopped sweating, the pain left and he was completely fine. Later that day the guy gave his life to Jesus.

One day I was pulling a cart with a couple hundred pounds of water on it, when the cart rolled up on the back of my ankle. I heard a pop, and I went down. By the time I got home that evening, I couldn't put any weight on that ankle. Me and my mom stood in the kitchen and prayed, commanding all the pain and swelling to leave. After we prayed, I stepped back on the bad ankle, which at this point was no longer bad. I began to jump up and down on it completely healed.

I was a manager for this company, and I had an employee who kept calling off of work. When she called off, I would have to do both her job and mine. I asked her, "Why do you call off so often, is there something wrong? She told me that she had bleeding ulcers and when they were flaring up she was in extreme pain and nausea. I asked her to sit down. I then prayed for her and told every ulcer to leave her body and for her stomach lining to be healed. The remainder of the time she worked there I don't think she ever called off from work again. God had healed her stomach.

I had another coworker who had an abscessed tooth and was in extreme pain. I put my hand on his shoulder and began to pray and this customer walks up and puts her hand on his other shoulder. It was pretty awesome. The Lord healed him and all the pain left.

I used to work at a grocery store. One day while working, I noticed a woman limp into my department. I approached her to ask her what was going on. She told me that she needed to have two total knee replacements. I asked her if I could pray for her. I prayed and then I told her that by the time she made it to the register to pay for her groceries all the pain would be gone. Later that day, I was paying for a loaf of bread when the girl working the register asked if I had prayed for a lady earlier. I told her, "yes. Why?" She told me, "some lady came up here and kept going on and on about some guy who had prayed for her in the produce section. And that all the pain in her knees was gone."

A couple weeks before this, a man came through my section in a wheelchair. I asked him what was going on? He told me that he needed a total knee replacement in one of his knees. I prayed for him and he left. A couple of weeks later he walked up to me. Yes, *walked* up to me. He told me that the day after I prayed for him, he realized that the pain in his knee was gone and he could walk.

I was at church one time when I saw a lady sitting gritting her teeth with her eyes closed. I tried to ask her what was going on but couldn't get anything out of her. The pain was so severe. I asked her husband who was with her what was wrong? He told me she had a herniated disk in her back. I prayed for and then told her to stand up and bend over and touch her toes. She was reluctant at first, but eventually got up and as she was going down to her toes, her eyes opened. She was in complete shock as she realized that she had absolutely no pain in her back anymore. Tears started to come down her face as she thanked God for healing her.

At another service, I had just finished speaking and a guy walked up to talk to me. I went to shake his hand and he pulled back. He then said that his hand was broken. I asked to see his hand. I gently held his hand in my hands as I prayed over it. I commanded all pain to leave and for the break to mend. I then told him to shake my hand. He reached out and began to shake my hand. As he shook it, his grip began to get tighter and tighter until he was squeezing my hand pretty hard. The Lord had completely healed his hand.

I once drove to a young lady's house with my friend. The young lady's mom had reached out to me because her daughter had Crohn's disease and was suffering from severe anxiety. Me and my friend began to pray for her. She said that she felt a heat in her stomach and then it traveled up her body to her head. She was completely healed and set free. The anxiety went away, as well as the Crohn's disease. I talked to her years later and she was still healed and free.

I was standing in the front of the church one day when a girl walked up to me crying. She had a baby daughter in one of those front body carriers. She asked if I remembered her. I told her, "I'm so sorry but I don't." She then began to tell me that she and her husband had come up to me the year before for prayer because they were unable to have children. She said that she just wanted to come up to show me her baby girl, whom she had named Hope.

One time I was leaving the grocery store when I saw this guy limping to his car. I went over to him and asked him what was going on with his ankle. He told me that he twisted it really bad the day before while working out. I asked if I could pray for him. He told me no, that he had someone pray for it earlier that day. When I got back to my car the Holy Spirit said, "I want you to go pray for that guy." I told Him, "I already asked and he said no."

The Holy Spirit replied, "Don't give up so easily." I got back out of the car and ran up to the guy before he drove off. I told him, "Sir I know that you told me that you didn't want prayer, but I'm really feeling led to pray for you and I believe the Lord is going to heal you right now in the parking lot." He was like "Okay" so I prayed for him and told him to walk on the ankle. As he began to walk, he looked up and asked "Who are you? What just happened?" I told him "I'm nobody, I just love Jesus and He loves you. He healed your ankle."

I was at the hospital one time to pray for a guy because he had a small hole in one in his intestines. When he ate, food was leaking into his body and basically poisoning him. Me and some friends prayed for him and it wasn't long before he was eating solid food again.

Another time I was in the hospital to pray for a guy who had cancer in his body. It had gotten bad. I think it had either gotten into his bones or his blood. Me and several friends prayed for him. The doctor really didn't have much hope of him surviving. I saw him a couple months later at church and now here it is years later and he is still living and doing fine.

Another time I was asked by a friend to go and pray for a guy who was in the hospital. We went and when we walked into the room it was not a good sight. The guy was burning up with a fever and there weren't any nurses around. You could hear the death rattle in his chest. He'd had a stroke. He was deaf at this point and could only see out of one eye, as the other eye was filmed over and all white. The doctors said that he would not walk out of that room alive. My friend and I prayed and the fever broke. Then, we began to praise God and I got down near his face and I said, "You will live and not die." About the third time I said this, the guy's eyes shot open. He sat and stared at me.

It was actually kind of freaky, but very encouraging. My friend then called his name and he turned to look at her. She said "can you hear me?" He shook his head yes. Then she said, "You will live and not die." He shook his head yes and then passed back out. Me and my friend looked at each other and knew that it was done. It had broken and he would recover. About one week after we prayed, the man left that hospital and went back home. The same hospital that said he will never leave this room alive. Unfortunately, months after this man went home, for unknown reasons he passed away. It was unexpected, as the man was gaining back strength and lost abilities from the stroke. I'll never forget that day though, when the power of God hit his body and his eyes shot open. We are called to bring light and life into situations that the world calls hopeless.

I once prayed for a friend who had fallen and broken her wrist the week before. The doctors had put a titanium plate in her wrist and a couple pins and screws. The following week after prayer, she had to go back to the doctor because the swelling had gone down and they wanted to put a smaller cast on. When she got there, they did an x-ray. The results came back and they told her that she wouldn't have to get another cast put on. Then they told her that she would be able to begin physical therapy that day if she wanted. Not long after this, she was about a year ahead of schedule strength-wise and with range of motion.

I was once at a donut shop buying a cup of coffee when I saw a guy in the parking lot with a back brace on. I ran out and asked him what was wrong?

He told me that he'd had back pain for a long time because of his work. I asked if I could pray. He said *yes,* so I prayed for him and God completely healed him. He then gave his heart to the Lord.

One day I had just finished eating lunch at Panera Bread when I walked out and got in my car. I had just started my car when the Holy Spirit said, "I want you to pray for that lady." An older lady had just gotten out of her car. I watched her walk in front of my car as I was debating in my mind whether I had really heard the Lord or if I was just imagining things. Really, I was thinking, *my car is already in reverse with my foot on the brake, do I throw it back into park to pray for this lady?*

As I was sitting there thinking about this, the lady literally fell-out in front of my car. I throw the car into park and jump out of the car. As I get to her she is unconscious. I immediately begin to pray for her as her daughter runs from around the other side of the car. Someone yells out "call for an ambulance!" I continue to pray for her not really paying attention to the people around me in panic. I rebuked the spirit of death and as soon as I got those words out of my mouth the lady's eyes shot open. Once again freaky, but very encouraging.

The Holy Spirit then told me that she needed to eat, as she hadn't eaten in a long time. I asked her daughter when the last time she ate was. She replied that she has no idea, since her mother was in a nursing home and they didn't force her to eat. They would just come in and take her plate, even if she hadn't eaten a single bite. The daughter told me "sometimes she goes long periods of time without eating and nobody knows when the last time she ate was." I then told the daughter to give her something to eat and I said that she would be fine. About this time the ambulance was showing up, so I got out of the way and left.

One day I was getting a haircut when the stylist winced in pain. I asked her what was wrong and she told me that she had back pain. I asked if I could pray for her when she was done. When we prayed nothing changed in her condition. After praying a second time and nothing happening, I asked her if one of her legs was shorter than the other? She said she didn't know so I asked her to sit down in a chair in the waiting room. She went and sat down and sure enough one leg was about an inch and a half shorter than the other. I then commanded the shorter leg to grow out. As it began to grow out, the other customers in the waiting room who were waiting to get their haircut became very curious, stretching their necks to their full extent to try and see what was happening. After the leg grew out. The lady stood up and the pain in her back was gone.

One time we were at a facility ministering to troubled teens, when a kid who had a metal plate in his hand came up to us. We asked if we could pray for him. After we prayed for him, we asked him to move his hand around to see if he could tell any difference in range of motion or flexibility. As he moved it around and went to touch where the metal had been, as he could normally feel it because it poked out a little, he could no longer find the metal in his hand anymore. He could now move his hand in ways that he couldn't move it since they put the metal in.

Another time at a different facility, one of the counselors had a broken toe. She had one of those boots on to take the pressure off the toe. I prayed for her and then told her to take the boot off. She said, "every time I do that and put any pressure on it, I end up throwing up from the pain." I told her it would be ok. She then took off the boot. I told her to put a little pressure on it. As she did, she realized there was no pain in the toe. She put a little more pressure on it and began to take a few steps. She then pressed the toe with her finger and to her amazement, she still felt no pain.

A guy that I knew called me one day to see if I could come over and pray for his mom. She'd had back pain for years and was scheduled to go in to have back surgery. I went over to the house and prayed for her. The pain almost completely went away and she gained back range of motion and flexibility that she had not had in a long time.

One summer I was snorkeling with my family and towards the end of the trip my mom yelled out, "Dion your dad!" I look over and my dad is in the water and can't breathe. He gasps out, "Dion help." As I began to swim over to him, I heard the Holy Spirit say it was his heart. When I get over to him, I wrap my arms around him from the back and put my left hand on his heart. And sure enough, his heart was making a jerking type movement. I closed my eyes and I began to say the name of Jesus over and over again. I had only said it a few times when his heart stopped jerking. I kept saying the name of Jesus and then he took a deep breath and he could breathe again. I kept saying the name of Jesus and the peace of God that was resting on me went onto him and he relaxed in my arms. We then swam back to the boat and he was completely fine.

Jesus is so good! These are just a few of the times I have seen the Lord lovingly heal people. Over the years I've probably prayed for everything that you can think of. I've prayed for backs, knees, shoulders, hearts, kidneys, legs, necks, stomachs, cancer, eyes, ears, wrists, toes, lungs, and even birds. Wait, I definitely have to tell you about that one.

One day I was driving to the store when this small blue bird swooped down in front of my bumper. I knew that I had hit him. I pull the car over and walk back to him and sure enough he was lying there just limp in the middle of the road. I pick the little guy up and move him a little bit. I get no response. I get down on my knees there on the side of the road and pray for him. After about a minute of praying for him, I say, "I release resurrection life into your body." No sooner than I got those words out of my mouth, the bird stands up and shoots off my hand flying into the woods.

Jesus is life, and He brings life to all. Even the smallest of creatures. I want you to notice that almost none of the testimonies I shared were actually in a church or at a service. One or two of them were, but the majority of them weren't. They happened in my day to day life. God is not bound to a building. Does He heal people in a church building? Yes, of course, but He also wants to heal people everywhere we go. There is always somebody that needs healing in their body when we go out.

The question is, do you notice them? Do you believe that God wants to heal them if you would just go up to talk to them? People are a lot more open and receptive to prayer than you think. Do I get turned down sometimes; Yes. Do I get looked at like I'm crazy sometimes; Yes. Do I pray for some people and they don't get healed; Yes. But at the same time, I would have never have seen Jesus heal anybody if I never stepped out there.

CONCLUSION

I really enjoyed writing this book as the healing power of God has been a passion of mine since that day Jesus healed me all those years ago. Since then I have been blessed to see Jesus heal so many. Seeing the joy on the faces of those whom the Lord heals, always encourages me to continue to pursue the heart of God in this area. He loves us dearly and wants us to be healthy and whole. People just aren't themselves when they are going through sickness. It's a burden we were never meant to carry since Jesus carried it for us.

We are called to bring the gospel of Jesus Christ to the world and healing is a part of that gospel. When Jesus walked the earth, all who came to Him were healed. This tells me that Jesus wants people healed.

And the word says that He is the same yesterday, today, and forever. We just need to keep pressing in until the full expression of Jesus' life is manifesting through us. We are called to be like Him and we have been given the Holy Spirit to bring this about. Allow the Lord to stretch you and grow you in every area. He is faithful and He will do it. We just need to trust Him and follow Him where He leads.

I encourage you now that you have read this book to begin to step out in these different areas and pray for the sick. Trust the Holy Spirit to give you words of knowledge and words of wisdom when you need them. He is faithful and you can trust Him. Trust me, He wants that person Healed more than you do. Trust and believe in the finished work of Jesus. He paid a heavy price for people to be healed. If you need healing in your body continue to read through and meditate on the truths revealed in this book until you've been made whole. Then go out there and teach others.

Not only have I seen a lot of people healed through these truths, but I too myself have been healed through them. Remember it's not the truths that heal you though. It's Jesus who heals you. It's His presence. Whether it's through the word, through worship, through communion, or through prayer, it's all the Lord. Even when He heals others through us, it's still Him. He is Jehovah Rapha: the Lord who heals. He has blessed us with the Holy Spirit, so we too can pray for the sick. Remember what He told me that day, "The hem of My garment, is the hem of your garment." Let us step out there believing in the God of miracles who still heals today.

Luke: 6:19 "And the whole multitude sought to touch Him, for the power went out of Him and He healed them all."

ABOUT THE AUTHOR

DION DIMOLA is a current resident of Orlando, Florida. There he spends his days chasing after the heart of God with an amazing family of Jesus-loving *Jesus People*. His heart is to see people's lives radically changed by the presence and love of God. He wants the whole world to know Jesus and to come into an intimate relationship with the Lord. His passions are reading, writing, teaching, and talking about the Lord.

TO CONNECT WITH DION, VISIT:

DIONDIMOLA.COM